Sunisa Lee

CHERRY LAKE PRESS

Published in the United States of America by Cherry Lake Publishing Group
Ann Arbor, Michigan
www.cherrylakepublishing.com

Reading Adviser: Beth Walker Gambro, MS, Ed., Reading Consultant, Yorkville, IL
Book Designer: Jennifer Wahi
Illustrator: Jeff Bane

Photo Credits: © Gang Liu/Shuttershock, 5; © CandyRetriever/Shuttershock, 7; © Master1305/Shuttershock, 9; © Alex Emanuel Koch/Shuttershock, 11; © BUENAFOTO/Shuttershock, 13; © A.RICARDO/Shuttershock, 15, 17, 19, 21, 22, 23; Cover, 1, 12, 16, 18, Jeff Bane; Various frames throughout, © Shutterstock Images

Cherry Lake Press is an imprint of Cherry Lake Publishing Group.

Library of Congress Cataloging-in-Publication Data

Names: Loh-Hagan, Virginia, author. | Bane, Jeff, 1957- illustrator.
Title: Sunisa Lee / Virginia Loh-Hagan ; [illustrator: Jeff Bane].
Description: Ann Arbor, Michigan : Cherry Lake Publishing Group, [2023] | Series: My Itty-Bitty Bio | ATOS: Below 1.9. Word Count: 201 words .
Identifiers: LCCN 2022009928 | ISBN 9781668908853 (Hardcover) | ISBN 9781668910450 (Paperback) | ISBN 9781668912041 (eBook) | ISBN 9781668913635 (pdf)
Subjects: LCSH: Lee, Sunisa, 2003---Juvenile literature. | Women gymnasts--United States--Biography--Juvenile literature. | Women Olympic athletes--United States--Biography--Juvenile literature. | Olympic Games (32nd : 2021 : Tokyo, Japan)--Juvenile literature. | Hmong American women--United States--Biography--Juvenile literature. | Illustrated children's books.
Classification: LCC GV460.2.L44 L65 2023 | DDC 796.44092 [B]--dc23/eng/20220506
LC record available at https://lccn.loc.gov/2022009928

Printed in the United States of America
Corporate Graphics

About the author: When not writing, Dr. Virginia Loh-Hagan serves as the director of the Asian Pacific Islander Desi American (APIDA) Center at San Diego State University. She identifies as Chinese American and is committed to amplifying APIDA communities. She lives in San Diego with her very tall husband and very naughty dogs.

About the illustrator: Jeff Bane and his two business partners own a studio along the American River in Folsom, California, home of the 1849 Gold Rush. When Jeff's not sketching or illustrating for clients, he's either swimming or kayaking in the river to relax.

I was born in 2003 in Minnesota. I'm **Hmong**. My parents were **refugees**.

I have a big family. I have five **siblings**. They call me "Suni."

How would you describe your family?

I had a lot of energy. I was very active. I did flips on my bed. My parents put me in **gymnastics** when I was 6.

I started competing the following year. At age 8, I had already moved up three levels.

What do you love to do?

I worked hard. I practiced every day. Gymnastics is expensive. But my family still supported me. My father built me a wooden **beam** to practice on.

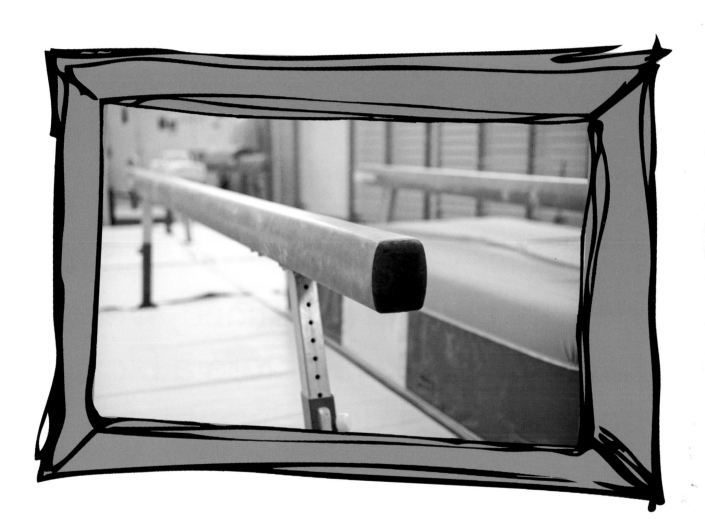

My father was in a bad accident. He was **paralyzed**. This happened 2 days before a big competition. I didn't want to compete. But he reminded me I had worked hard.

What challenges have you faced?

My hard work paid off. I was included in *Time* magazine's list of 100 most **influential** people.

I went to Japan in 2021.
I competed in the Olympic
Games. I won gold, silver,
and bronze medals!

My **legacy** continues. I'm the first Hmong American Olympian. I continue to inspire others.

What would you like to ask me?

2019

2000

Born
2003

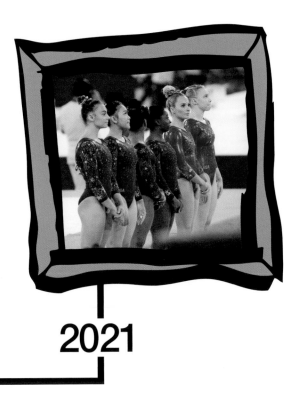

2021

2100

glossary

beam (BEEM) a thick wooden board used in gymnastics

gymnastics (jim-NAH-stiks) a sport involving physical exercises of strength and balance

Hmong (MUHNG) an ethnic group of Asia

influential (in-floo-EN-shuhl) having the power to cause change

legacy (LEH-guh-see) something handed down from one generation to another

paralyzed (PER-uh-lyzed) unable to move

refugees (reh-fyoo-JEES) people who flee to another place to escape danger or war

siblings (SIHB-lings) brothers or sisters

index